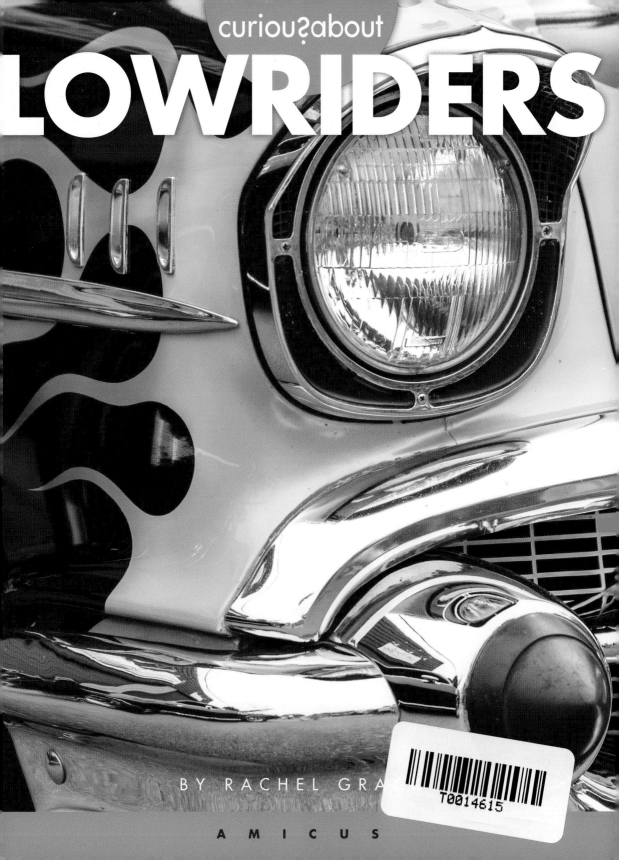

curiousabout

LOWRIDERS

BY RACHEL GRA

AMICUS

What are you

curious about?

CHAPTER THREE

3

On the Street

PAGE

18

Curious About is published by
Amicus
P.O. Box 227
Mankato, MN 56002
www.amicuspublishing.us

Editors: Gillia Olson and Alissa Thielges
Designer: Kathleen Petelinsek
Photo researcher: Bridget Prehn

Library of Congress Cataloging-in-Publication Data
Names: Koestler-Grack, Rachel A., 1973- author.
Title: Curious about lowriders / by Rachel Grack.
Description: Mankato : Amicus, 2023. | Series: Curious
about cool rides | Includes bibliographical references and
index. | Audience: Ages 6–9. | Audience: Grades 2–3.
Identifiers: LCCN 2020001123 (print) | LCCN 2020001124
(ebook) | ISBN 9781645491170 (library binding) | ISBN
9781681526843 (paperback) | ISBN 9781645491590 (pdf)
Subjects: LCSH: Lowriders—Juvenile literature. |
Automobiles—Customizing—Juvenile literature.
Classification: LCC TL255.2 .K64 2023 (print) | LCC TL255.2
(ebook) | DDC 629.222—dc23
LC record available at https://lccn.loc.gov/2020001123
LC ebook record available at https://lccn.loc.gov/2020001124

Photos © Shutterstock/Stefan Malloch cover, 1; Alamy/
Goddard New Era 4–5; Getty/Ted Soqui/Corbis 6–7; Historic
Vehicle Association 3, 8–9 (both), 20–21; Dreamstime/
Ldionisio 11 (top); Alamy/Goddard New Era 11 (blue); Getty/
Barcroft Media 2 (left), 11 (orange); Dreamstime/Smitty Smitty
11 (yellow); Shutterstock/Vlad Kochelaevskiy 12; Alamy/
Victor Korchenko 2 (right), 13; Alamy/Michael Wheatley
14–15; iStock/curtis_creative 16; Shutterstock/RTimages 17
(5-spoke); Shutterstock/ultrapok 17 (wire spoke); Pxfuel/Premium
Sport 17 (narrow wall); Pixabay/markus53 17 (wide wall);
PxHere 17 (spinner); Shutterstock/David Tran Photo 18-19

What are lowriders?

LOW AND SLOW

Lowriders are cars with very low bodies. The frames nearly touch the road. They have cool paint jobs and shiny wheels. Some even bounce! Lowriders are custom **cruising** cars. They go low and slow.

Lowriders can have flashy paint jobs.

When did lowriding start?

A 1950s lowrider drives in Los Angeles, California.

People started lowering cars in the 1940s. Mexican Americans liked the look. Lowriders became part of their **culture**. The cars stood out. They showed pride in Mexican history. Today, lowriders star in movies and music videos.

What kinds of cars become lowriders?

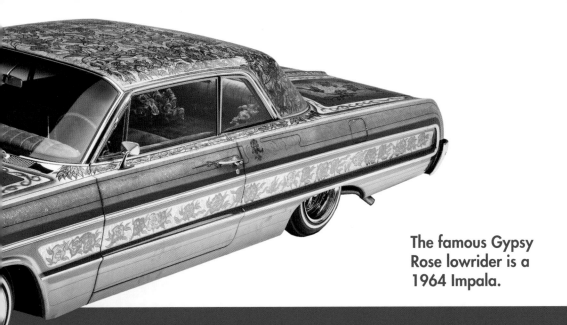

The famous Gypsy Rose lowrider is a 1964 Impala.

Almost any car can be one. Chevy Impalas from the 1960s are favorites. Their frames have space to add parts. The huge **fenders** fit all kinds of tires. The wide sides have big spaces for painting.

Why do lowriders all look so different?

Each lowrider is a work of art. Drivers become the artists. They use bright colors and detailed designs. They add **chrome** and gold. Some choose **pinstripes**. Others paint pictures about their family or beliefs. Their cars tell a story.

Flames are a common design.

DID YOU KNOW?
Lowriders usually have unique paint jobs.

CHAPTER TWO

How do you lower a car?

You change the **suspension**. This is where the wheels connect to the frame. Years ago, drivers cut down the suspension's springs to lower the car. Today, lowriders usually have air ride or **hydraulic** suspensions instead of springs. The car is raised and lowered with the push of a button.

The suspension holds the car up so it can move.

Lowrider suspensions are custom built.

What makes lowriders hop?

A lowrider makes one tire jump off the ground.

Hydraulic suspensions. These use liquid to raise and lower the car. They work fast. The car jumps! The lifts can tip cars in all directions. Cars look like they are dancing. Some lowrider shows even hold dance contests!

DID YOU KNOW?
The highest hop is 163.25 inches (414.65 cm). That's over 13 feet (4 m)!

Do lowriders have special tires?

Whitewall tires are popular on classic lowriders.

Drivers usually put on small tires. They make the car even lower. Most lowriders roll on narrow **whitewall tires**. Flashy, custom wheels hold the tires. Owners might also add **hubcaps** over the wheels. Some hubcaps spin on their own.

NARROW WHITEWALL TIRE

WIDE WHITEWALL TIRE

WIRE SPOKE WHEEL

5-SPOKE ALLOY WHEEL

SPINNER HUBCAPS

CHAPTER THREE

Are lowriders street safe?

Yes! Lowriders are for cruising, after all. They still need to follow the laws. Some states do not allow dark windows or colored lights. Cars cannot **scrape** the road. This might cause sparks.

A man drives his lowrider in a parade.

What's it like to drive one?

The inside of the Gypsy Rose lowrider is all pink.

Comfy and booming! Many lowriders have seats like couches. The seats might be covered in soft **velvet** or colored leather. Almost all have a good stereo. Music is a huge part of lowriding. Turn up the tunes and hop to the beat!

ASK MORE QUESTIONS

Are there any famous lowriders?

What does a lowrider contest look like?

Try a BIG QUESTION:
Imagine you had a lowrider. How would you paint it?

SEARCH FOR ANSWERS

Search the library catalog or the Internet.
A librarian, teacher, or parent can help you.

Using Keywords
Find the looking glass.

Keywords are the most important words in your question.

?

If you want to know about:

- famous lowrider cars, type: FAMOUS LOWRIDERS

- lowrider contests, type: LOWRIDER EVENTS

FIND GOOD SOURCES

Here are some good, safe sources you can use in your research.
Your librarian can help you find more.

Books
Lowriders by Matthew Doeden, 2019.

Lowriders by Thomas Adamson, 2019.

Internet Sites
¡Colores! Lowriders segment
*https://www.pbs.org/video/
colores-colores-july-16-2016/*
PBS is public television. It has fact-based, educational programming without many ads.

National Historic Vehicle Register
*https://www.hagerty.com/drivers-club/
my-garage/78598943/
national-historic-vehicle-register*
Check out some of the most historic vehicles in American history.

Every effort has been made to ensure that these websites are appropriate for children. However, because of the nature of the Internet, it is impossible to guarantee that these sites will remain active indefinitely or that their contents will not be altered.

SHARE AND TAKE ACTION

See some cool cars by going to a car show.
Ask a parent to see when a show will be near you. You might even have a lowrider show nearby.

Build your own hopping lowrider!
Buy a lowrider model car with a hop hydraulics kit. Ask an adult to help you put it together.

Draw a custom paint job for your lowrider.
You can use drawing paper. Don't forget the whole car can be used. What story would you tell with your car?

GLOSSARY

chrome Shiny silver metal.

cruising Driving around just for fun.

culture The ways of life, ideas, and traditions of a group of people.

fender The metal part of a car's body that hangs over the wheels.

hubcap A cover that fits over the wheel of a car.

hydraulic Having to do with liquid in motion.

pinstripes Thin striped designs on a car.

scrape To peel or scratch something with a sharp object.

suspension The system that connects wheels to a car's frame.

velvet A soft cloth with short raised fibers on one side.

whitewall tire A tire with a white stripe on the side.

INDEX

About the Author

Rachel Grack has been editing and writing children's books since 1999. She lives on a ranch in Arizona. Hot cars have always fired her up! At one time, she even owned a street rod—a 1965 Ford Galaxie 500. She loved cruising with the windows down. This series refueled her passion for cool rides!